Make Your Sma
By Conrad Jaege
ISBN: 978

v
© Deep Web Gu
Updated March 2017
www.alanpearce.com

Table of Contents

5 - Introduction
12 - **1.** Clear Out, Load Up, Lock Down, Run Silent
14 - **2.** Keeping out the Spies
18 - **3.** High-Level Threats
28 - **4.** Counter-Intrusion
34 - **5.** Accessing Hidden Networks
41 ----Using Tor
44 ----Entry Points
60 - **6.** Secure Communication
63 - **7.** Secret Messaging
65 - **8.** Usenet Newsgroups
69 - **9.** Portable Apps
72 - **10.** 007 Apps
79 - **11.** IP Cameras
81 - **12. How to Search More Effectively**
Recommended Links
Further Reading

Disclaimer

This book is for educational purposes only. In no way is it the intention of the author, publishers or distributors to encourage anyone to do anything illegal. The author, publishers and distributors accept no liability for anything that happens in any way connected with the reading, possession or use of this book.
Don't even think about it.

A technical aside

The Deep Web addresses marked **<!>** listed here can only be opened with Tor-Firefox browser, which you will learn to configure later.

Free, open source software is generally preferable to the paid-for variety because it can be tested by developers and any logging devices or backdoors can be identified.

Be alert that no single system or piece of software is 100% secure or safe.

Recommended links are given throughout the book and at the end.

Introduction

The smartphone in your pocket can easily be turned into a high-tech spy tool and counter-surveillance device to rival anything that Ian Fleming's Q might have dreamt up.

You can communicate secretly, browse the web anonymously, access the Deep Web and hidden networks, view banned content, download privately, and continue using Twitter and Facebook if their services are ever blocked locally. You can even take over and control many public and private security cameras.

Conversely, mobile devices are not secure unless you make them so. If somebody wants to know where you are at this precise moment, your smartphone or tablet will tell them – even if they are turned off.

Mobile espionage, long the preserve of law enforcement and specialized investigators, has now evolved into a fully-fledged cybercrime industry. In 2011, Kaspersky Labs detected nearly 5,300 new malicious programs for all mobile platforms. By the end of 2012, the number exceeded six million – the vast majority aimed at Android. Today, that number is almost impossible to count.

When it comes to securing your system, there are several concerns – ad networks, cybercriminals, stalkers, malicious trolls, law enforcement, intelligence agencies and corporate spies – and they all use similar techniques. Generally, they do this by so-called "social engineering", the art of playing on peoples' gullibility or natural desire to please. They do this by enticing people to open email attachments or by following links to malicious websites where malware will instantly load much in the same way as a conventional cookie.

Cybercriminals make the most of news events and consumer trends to draw people to a webpage where malware will automatically plant itself in the computer, known as a "drive-by download". Malware can also be surreptitiously planted in legitimate websites to infect even the wary. These are known as "watering hole" attacks.

Within hours of the Boston marathon bombing, the spammers were sending out emails and Twitter links seemingly from CNN which sent users to sites compromised by a Blackhole Exploit Kit where many were infected by Trojans, backdoors, infostealers or rootkits. The same thing happens around most major news stories. And it's not just the gullible public who fall prey. Seasoned journalists are regularly sucked in with the apparent deaths of celebrities or by looming sex scandals.

Another growing threat is Ransomware, which locks a device until a "fine" is paid. Infections often come via legitimate but compromised websites and advertisements where hackers have managed to insert malicious coding. Victims suddenly find their screen frozen and a fake warning from the FBI or local law enforcement saying they have been downloading illegal content. Even more unnerving, the perpetrators occasionally include a mug shot from the victim's own webcam. This malware is extremely hard to remove and, needless to say, once a fine has been paid the device stays locked. If you should ever fall victim, contact *No More Ransom*.

The majority of malware comes hidden inside seemingly harmless apps which run in the background and collect data all day long. Malicious programs have been detected in apps on Google Play and the App Store for iOS. Intelligence agencies are known to "piggy-back" off this data and add it to the pool of profiles.

They will track your locations, browsing and downloads, and collaborate with other running apps to build up a detailed profile. Some will intercept incoming calls or activate the microphone. Many apps harvest contacts, some collect passwords, while others send secret messages to premium-rate numbers, running up your charges.

Most apps are free or very cheap because developers make their money by allowing in ad networks and other malevolent parties. Be alert when an app asks permission to use your current location – many don't bother to ask – and never give out email addresses or any personal details.

Additionally, any hostile actor or stalker can pay around US$50 a month for a tracking program that they then hide inside the target device. It takes just a few minutes for someone with your device in their hands to download and install the tracking program.

These programs are ostensibly sold for parents to keep track of their children or for bosses to keep an eye on staff but, of course, anyone with any intention can buy one. They can then access every aspect of your online activity, including stealing your passwords. They can even prevent outgoing calls to the police or anybody they select. They are also virtually undetectable. If you suspect you may be a victim, begin by placing a sticker over the webcam and then consider re-setting the device to its factory defaults.

The key here is to prevent malware from entering your devices in the first place. Never open any attachment that you are unsure of. Install in all your devices a good free anti-spyware program such as Avast. This will alert you whenever somebody sends you a malicious email attachment. You can also use the program to scan suspicious files. Equally, never follow any link that you are unsure of, especially so if the address is a shortened URL. Again, Avast should warn you when you arrive at a suspicious website and prevent unauthorized downloads.

1. Clear Out, Load Up, Lock Down, Run Silent

Begin by clearing out from your smartphone and tablet any unwanted or unused programs, especially the games.
Then install a good anti-spyware program such as the free version of Avast. Also install a VPN (Virtual Private Network) to keep you safe when using public Wi-Fi points. Hotspot Shield comes in both free and Elite versions for all devices.

Install a secure messaging app. We recommend the free version of Open Whisper Systems Signal and encourage your friends and contacts to do the same. This will prevent anyone listening in on your calls or reading your messages.

Always cover your webcam – on all of your digital devices. These cameras are never safe and can very easily be tapped into, opening your life to deep scrutiny.

You should also pay attention to the devices' *Settings* and limit the amount of information you give away. See Counter-Intrusion.

This is your starting point. In order to stay safe in the digital world it is important to understand how your potential adversaries operate and then to take appropriate counter measures. The pages below will show you how.

2. Keeping out the Spies

Intelligence agencies and law enforcement use malware, one example being FinSpy, which they send to people in spoof emails, allowing agents to take control of smartphones and other devices, intercepting Skype calls, turning on cameras and recording keystrokes. Researchers have found FinSpy running on 36 servers worldwide. Cyber-criminals use the same techniques, although they are often less sophisticated.

As scary as this might seem, dodgy redirects and 'drive-bys' can be pre-empted with a good anti-virus program (see Counter-Intrusion).

To avoid infection via email, disable HTML in your email program via the *Settings* tab. Look for and untick *Display attachments online* or tick *View message body as...plain text*.

Never open attachments or click on links if you are unsure of their origin. If you must open a suspicious attachment, first scan it with a good anti-spyware program. Be especially alert for any *.apk* attachments and destroy them immediately. However, malware can be hidden inside most digital files.

Equally, be aware of social media posts with enticing links, many of which are often shortened so you don't know where you are heading. Short URLs can be enlarged with a URL enlarger. If you are still suspicious, check out the address with Web Inspector which will scan for malware.

Additionally, law enforcement may oblige the service provider to remotely reprogram a phone's air card allowing for precision tracking. They may also set up spoof cellphone towers, luring you to pass through their network first. This technique, generically known as 'stingray' or IMSI catcher, allows agents to spoof a legitimate cell tower and trick the smartphone into connecting directly to the stingray. These are now being installed on drones to suck up all traffic at specific locations. Criminals use similar techniques in popular Wi-Fi points using spyware that costs around $100. Always employ a VPN to avoid these techniques.

It is also advisable to secure your home and office wireless networks. The simplest solution is to change the administrator password for the wireless router. Hackers can look-up the manufacturer's default password and easily break in, intercepting all the data you send and receive. You should also refer to the router's handbook and switch off SSID (Service Set Identifier) broadcasting and change the default SSID name to something not easily identifiable. Additionally, always enable encryption in your connection settings, preferably WPA or else WEP encryption.

3. High-Level Threats

While some people believe the Internet has set them free, others are waking up to the fact that we are all voluntarily plugged into the finest surveillance apparatus ever devised. But let's be clear about this: everything we do in the digital world is open to scrutiny by suspicious minds because that's the way intelligence agencies work. If they didn't make use of this amazing opportunity, they wouldn't be very good at their job.

All sophisticated security services monitor Internet traffic within their own countries. The US monitors *all* Internet traffic if it passes through US-owned 'processing services', which the bulk of it does. Legally, just the bare bones of the communications are monitored – the who sent what and when. But, although they may not be open about this, many agencies are now looking directly into the message itself, looking for the expected and the unexpected in all our online communications and activities.

But don't suppose actual agents are used for such mundane tasks. Algorithms of stunning complexity analyze literally every word. And, when certain triggers are pulled, the surveillance moves up a notch and so on until it enters the physical world. According to the US Government Accountability Office, back in 2004 there were 199 separate data mining programs being run by 16 Federal agencies on the look-out for suspicious activity.

By 2010, *The Washington Post* concluded after a two-year investigation that there were around 1,200 government agencies and 1,900 private companies working on counter-terrorism, homeland security and other domestic intelligence programs from within thousands of secret data processing sites and "fusion centers" that constitute an "alternative geography of the United States".

The National Security Agency intercepts and stores the data from nearly 3 billion emails and other communications each day in its attempts to predict crime in what it terms the "paradigm of prevention" or "predictive policing"; and each day more than 1,600 people have their names added to the FBI's terrorism watchlist.

Agencies like the CIA collect all the data they can and then they store it indefinitely. If they ever need to join the dots, it helps to have all the dots from the past to draw upon.
Tracking people in cyberspace is child's play, especially when more than half of all Internet users have a page on Facebook. Big Data – Social, Mobile and Cloud – has altered the flow of information, overtaking traditional media. With commercially-available software like Raytheon's social media data mining tool RIOT, simply enter a person's name and up pops a colorful graph showing where they have been, who they met and what they all look like. It then predicts their future movements.

If they have someone in their sights, the bad guys then insert malware into the smartphone and take remote control; listening in on conversations, intercepting SMS and VoIP calls, and noting everything.

Nothing escapes their attention. There is a school of thought that the most successful companies got where they are today with a little outside help.

Imagine starting a service where millions of people will openly detail their lives and speak their minds. Then imagine being approached by an organization that would like to help you become a global brand. All you have to do in return is add a 'backdoor' allowing them direct access to the real names and physical addresses of everybody who signs up.

If you don't play ball, well, your business will go nowhere and you might find that suddenly your credit cards don't work and then things begin to spiral downwards for you. It's not really an option. You build a backdoor. That's the theory.

When Briton Leigh Van Bryan, 26, planned a vacation to Hollywood, he tweeted friends that he planned to "destroy America", meaning in London-slang that he was going to have a jolly good time. The Department of Homeland Security didn't see it that way and were ready and waiting for him when he landed at Los Angeles Airport. He was handcuffed, interrogated for hours, locked in the cells overnight and unceremoniously deported.

They knew everything about him except what he was actually talking about. Algorithms may be smart but they just don't get the nuances. It's the little things like this which can set a suspicious mind off on a very deep investigation or drag you quickly off to a window-less cell.

It's the same with email. If you don't believe that every word you write is scrutinized, try typing into an email the words, *bomb kill President Tuesday* and see how long it takes for them to come and get you.

Trackers are everywhere. Pay a visit to Twitter or Facebook and they will instantly plant thousands of little robots that follow you around, noting everything you do.

To scoop up everybody else, the agencies channel users through a series of 'black boxes' or inspection points scattered around the net which then read everything that passes through them, analyzing it, logging it, storing it for deeper examination, or marking it for further attention.

With this so-called Deep Packet Inspection (DPI), all Internet traffic can be read, copied or modified, as can websites. DPI can also see who is uploading or downloading, what is inside and who is looking for it. Websites can be blocked and so can specific items within sites such as a particular video on YouTube.

Generally, ISPs and most governments can examine the 'header' of a message, seeing where it came from and where it's going, but they have not been able legally to peer inside. DPI has been used for years in the commercial world but only Tunisia, China, Iran and Kazakhstan legally use the system to curb dissidents.

The Community Comprehensive National Cybersecurity Initiative Data Center in Utah is now on-stream, capturing all communication globally, including the complete contents of private emails, cell phone calls and Internet searches, plus all the personal data trails from parking receipts, bank transfers, travel itineraries and bookstore purchases. Without DPI, the center would be meaningless.

But this is small-fry. The US – along with its Five Eyes cyber-partners Britain, Canada, Australia and New Zealand – taps directly into undersea and fiber optic cables as well as communications satellites, taking the data from the source. The result is that virtually everything which travels on the Surface Internet, and much else, is open to inspection.

Data storage is remarkably cheap and getting cheaper every year. Analyzing and storing it all is now a cost-effective reality and, once again, they would be failing as intelligence agencies if they didn't. The CIA proudly admits that "it is nearly within our grasp to compute on all human generated information."

Today everything is connected, everything communicates and everything is a sensor. Technology is moving so fast that even the major agencies can't keep up. Put all these things together and the inanimate becomes sentient; and suddenly the great dystopian fear is a reality.

And this is how they profile you. It's been happening for years in the commercial world. Only when you appear to step out of line, say the wrong thing or spend too long looking at a bad kind of wiki, will you become interesting to the suspicious minds.

But mistakes are easily made in a world overseen by computers and not so easily rectified as Mikey Hicks of New Jersey knows well. Every time he tries to fly, he is detained and thoroughly searched. Mikey is now 13 years old and has been on the No-Fly List since he was two.

As it turns out, the bad guys don't say *kill* or *bomb* in their emails or on Twitter. The terrorists and super-criminals can also hire the smartest brains in the IT world and they pay better.

According to the US National Academy of Sciences, whilst data mining may work in the commercial world, it simply isn't feasible to prevent atrocities because terrorists don't use a one size fits all model; they change and adapt their *modus operandi* as they go along, preventing the algorithms from picking out a pattern.

Curiously, governments and intelligence agencies know this, too.

4. Counter-Intrusion

There are many free and paid-for security options for every mobile operating device. Ironically, viruses are commonly hidden inside smartphone security software. Only install programs from the big names companies like Avast, AVG and Kaspersky, etc.

For Android users, a good free option is AVG Mobilation which protects against viruses, malware and spyware. It also identifies unsecure device settings and advises on how to fix them; ensures contacts, bookmarks and text messages are secure; checks media files for malicious software and security threats; guards against phishing; and offers anti-theft protection. Lost or stolen smartphones can be found via Google Maps, plus you can turn your phone's GPS on remotely and have the device send its location to you. You can also lock your phone remotely.

For iOS, the Anti-Virus & Malware Scanner does much the same as AVG Mobilation but additionally lets you scan files on remote locations such as Dropbox and web servers. Trend Micro also offers good mobile security for Android.

Lookout protects iOS or Android devices from unsecure Wi-Fi networks, malicious apps, fraudulent links, etc. You can also use it to back up your contacts by scheduling automatic backups and then accessing the information online, or using it to restore your device in case of a crash or data loss. If you lose your phone, Lookout can locate it on Google Maps – even if the GPS is off and the phone is on silent.

Pry-Fi for Android confounds eavesdroppers by putting out a false MAC address. Even if your Wi-Fi is turned off, most modern Android devices will still broadcast your identifying MAC address, announcing who and where you are. According to the developers "Pry-Fi comes with a *War* mode, which when enabled tries to make your Android device appear like dozens of people."

Do not let your mobile devices out of your sight and this includes leaving them unattended in hotel rooms. If, at airports or border crossings etc, the authorities insist on taking your device away, there is the possibility that they may scan the memory or plant malware inside.

With laptops and tablets, it is a good idea to place a sticker over any opening parts so you can see if the device has been tampered with. A very good alternative is to apply a coating of glitter nail polish and then take a photo of it with your smartphone. The glitter in the polish provides a unique pattern that cannot be replicated and which can later be compared to the photo. Additionally, be sure to thoroughly run an anti-spyware program on the device as soon as possible after recovery.

When choosing a password, select a memorable phrase rather than an actual word that can be found in a dictionary. For example, I Like Lots Of Vinegar On My Fish And Chips can be written as ILLOVOMFAC. You could add to this numbers and non-alphanumeric characters and a mix of upper and lower case. If you have a UK-English keyboard, use the £ symbol for its rarity value. Therefore, £ILloVomFaC! could stand as your basic passphrase and then add on an identifier such as £ILloVomFaC!rain for Amazon, using rain to help you remember because the Amazon is a tropical rain forest.

Put a security code on your smartphone in addition to the SIM code and engage the auto-locking feature.

- Disable network connections and switch off bridging connections. Do not broadcast the Bluetooth device name and disable automated peer-to-peer Wi-Fi connections.
- Turn off Geotagging and GPS location via *Settings*.

- Whenever possible, access 3G or 4G networks in preference to free Wi-Fi services.
- Do not store sensitive files on the phone's internal storage. Encrypt data or hide in a secret compartment.
- Enable remote-find or remote-wipe features.
- Avoid 'Jailbreaking' any device – the act of removing limitations through software or hardware exploits.
- Do not connect personal devices to the office network or computer.
- Avoid free charging points.
- Watch for unauthorized charges, rapidly-depleting battery and unusual text messages.

If you link your smartphone to your car's on-board computer, be sure to regularly delete sensitive information, contacts and travel history.

Update models regularly to keep the operating system in line with security enhancements.

Remove battery or leave your phone behind when meeting contacts, etc. If meeting in a group, do not all remove the battery at the same time as this appears ultra-suspicious to anyone observing any members of the group. The battery cannot be removed from an iPhone but it can be run down until completely flat and then resurrected with a portable battery. Remove the sim card, too.

5. Accessing Hidden Networks

Tell someone that you know how to go off-radar on the Internet and as a rule they won't believe you. They imagine the intelligence agencies have state-of-the-art technology and can see everything you do. This is only partially true. They do have amazing technology but they can only see things if they know where to look. Down in the Deep Web, by mixing and matching different technologies, you can stay out of sight and make it seriously difficult for any adversary to locate you.
Simply put, the Deep Web encompasses everything that the conventional search engines can't find. Google may index around 16 billion pages but it only seeks out those that want to be found or have conventional addresses that end in *.com* or *.org*, etc. It skims the surface and offers up the most popular results.

Largely unnoticed by most users, the Internet has been quietly evolving into a vast un-indexed data store. As a result, this Deep Web is so mind-bogglingly huge – some say more than 5,000 times the size of the Surface Internet – that it is both easy to get lost and to stay hidden.

Within this Deep Web are an unknown number of hidden networks; one of which is Tor, a dark world of anonymity. Here, people may communicate secretly and securely away from the attention of governments and corporations, scrutinize top secret papers before WikiLeaks gets them, and discuss all manner of unconventional topics.

Ironically, Tor – which stands for The Onion Router – was set up with funds from the US military at the start of the Millennium as a means of covert communication. So dark and murky is it, that other agencies now use it, as do most serious criminals and journalists, aid workers and activists.

Tor has its own websites, chat rooms, forums, blogs, file hosts, social networks and other features of the Surface Web. It is very easy to run into arms dealers, drug cartels, spies, pedophiles, kidnappers, slave traders and terrorists. You can buy top grade marijuana direct from the grower, trade stolen credit cards, buy the names and addresses of rape victims, or arrange the murder of an inquisitive reporter or pernickety judge – and then pay for it all with the Deep Web's own currency, the untraceable BitCoin.

Generally, this is why the Deep Web has a bad reputation. But it has positive aspects, too. There are many journalists who use Deep Web tools like the PrivacyBox to communicate securely with whistle blowers and dissidents. Aid agencies use similar techniques to keep their staff safe inside of authoritarian regimes.

The Deep Web is also a largely-unknown research and information resource, a goldmine of knowledge lodged in the databases of academic institutions, small businesses and corporations, research establishments, galleries and governments. If you know the right entry points, you can mine a rich seam of multimedia files, images, software and documents that you cannot find on the Surface Web. (See 'Deep Search – How to Explore the Internet More Effectively' to learn how to search the 'hidden' Internet).

You can take your smartphone or tablet onto Tor and keep everything off-radar using apps for Android and iOS with access to both Deep and Surface Webs, plus PM and email without being monitored or blocked. However, you will not be able to access certain sites this way if they insist on JavaScript.

Additionally, the free Tor/Firefox bundle is available for most operating systems. This is safe and easy to install. Simply follow the on-screen instructions and a gateway to the Deep Web can be configured in minutes with no special skills.

In certain situations, such as a demonstrations and riots, Tor-enabled devices can still connect to social networks and websites which may be blocked by the government. However, most social networks make heavy use of JavaScript which will give your identity away but Twitter does have a mobile facility as does Facebook Mobile which do not use JavaScript and can, therefore, be accessed anonymously.

Tor works by diverting your traffic through a worldwide volunteer network of servers. This conceals your location and your activities, effectively hiding you among all the other users. Tor works by encrypting and re-encrypting data multiple times as it passes through successive relays. This way the data cannot be unscrambled in transit.

Tor does have its flaws and should not be considered completely safe. Although your IP address is concealed, a digital fingerprint can linger allowing someone accessing your local network – a Wi-Fi provider or an ISP working with criminals or law enforcement – to glean some idea of your activities.

However, the waters can be mudded for any eavesdropper by requesting more than one site at a time or by downloading more than one item simultaneously, and by regularly re-setting the *Use a new identity* facility on the Tor control panel.

Certain plug-ins will not work on the Tor browser such as Flash, RealPlayer and QuickTime as they can be manipulated into revealing an IP address.
Once loaded, the browser will display a very basic-looking webpage (the Deep Web resembles the Surface Web circa 1996) and the words:

Congratulations. Your browser is configured to use Tor.

Please refer to the Tor website for further information about using Tor safely. You are now free to browse the Internet anonymously.

You are now anonymous and free to explore the Tor network or branch off to the Surface Web.

Using Tor

Rather like time travel, this level of the Internet appears much as it did in the very early days, including the lengthy wait while pages load. There are no frills or flashy graphics, just simple text and images.

On Tor, people communicate secretly and securely. Whistle blowers and dissidents, activists and journalists, aid-workers and academics, criminals and terrorists, all carry on their day-to-day activities.

Top secret papers are posted here, as are guides and wikis for every type of activity, legal and otherwise; and all manner of unconventional views are expressed. Here you can lurk hidden and surreptitiously store any amount of data for free.

This is pioneer territory with very few settlers; perhaps 500,000 daily users at best compared to the 3 billion plus who stay up top. Some of the natives are hostile because they would rather keep the place to themselves. Others are friendly because they know more users mean more people to hide amongst.

Deep Websites can disappear or fail to load from time to time. If you have difficulty opening a particular page, just try again later and it may reappear. The addresses given below were active at the time of publication. However, action by various law enforcement agencies and other factors has meant that many Tor websites have been taken offline.

However, be warned that there are many scams on the Tor network. While it is perfectly possible to buy all manner of drugs here, those offering goods such as iPhones and tablets at "unbelievable" prices are truly offering something that is too good to be true. It's always a good idea to check reviews on forums before making any purchase. The more reputable business sites have their accompanying forums. A good starting point for reliable markets is DeepDotWeb.com.

Entry Points

The Hidden Wiki <!>
http://zqktlwi4fecvo6ri.onion/wiki/Main_Page often described as the hub of the Deep Web, this is the best starting point for new-comers. Here you can find lists of other hidden networks and links to black market goods and financial services, file hosts, blogs, forums, political groups and whistle-blowing boards. Beware that many of the traders here are pure scammers, so be very cautious before parting with any money. The wiki is available in 17 languages. Mirror sites: <!> http://wikitjerrta4qgz4.onion/ and <!> http://zqktlwi4fecvo6ri.onion/wiki/index.php/Main_Page. The Uncensored Hidden Wiki can be found at <!> http://gxamjbnu7uknahng.onion/wiki/index.php/Main_Page
Tor*Links* <!> torlinkbgs6aabns.onion links directory where you can add your own links and set up a Deep Website.
OnionDir <!> http://dirnxxdraygbifgc.onion/ Tor link directory.

OnionList <!>
http://jh32yv5zgayyyts3.onion/ Onion link list and directory.
ParaZite Links List <!>
http://kpynyvym6xqi7wz2.onion/links.html
Onion URL Repository <!>
http://32rfckwuorlf4dlv.onion/
TorWiki <!>
http://torwikignoueupfm.onion/index.php?title=Main_Page

Deep Search Engines — Tor has a number but none are in any way comprehensive:
Ahmia Tor Search https://ahmia.fi
Torch <!>
http://xmh57jrzrnw6insl.onion/
DuckDuckGo Search Engine <!>
http://3g2upl4pq6kufc4m.onion/

Marketplace Drugs <!>
https://www.deepdotweb.com/marketplace-directory/categories/top-markets/

Misc <!> We take no responsibility for the trustworthiness or reliability of the following Onion sites. Equally, they may not always be available.

http://e266al32vpuorbyg.onion/bookmarks.php - Dark Nexus
http://5plvrsgydwy2sgce.onion/ - Seeks Search
http://2vlqpcqpjlhmd5r2.onion/ - Gateway to Freenet
http://nlmymchrmnlmbnii.onion/ - Is It Up?
http://kpynyvym6xqi7wz2.onion/links.html - ParaZite
http://wiki5kauuihowqi5.onion/ - Onion Wiki
http://torwikignoueupfm.onion/index.php?title=Main_Page - Tor Wiki
http://kpvz7ki2v5agwt35.onion - The Hidden Wiki
http://idnxcnkne4qt76tg.onion/ - Tor Project: Anonymity Online
http://torlinkbgs6aabns.onion/ - TorLinks
http://jh32yv5zgayyyts3.onion/ - Hidden Wiki .Onion Urls
http://wikitjerrta4qgz4.onion/ - Hidden Wiki - Tor Wiki

http://xdagknwjc7aaytzh.onion/ - Anonet Webproxy
http://3fyb44wdhnd2ghhl.onion/wiki/index.php?title=Main_Page - All You're Wiki - clone of the clean hidden wiki that went down with freedom hosting
http://3fyb44wdhnd2ghhl.onion/ - All You're Base
http://j6im4v42ur6dpic3.onion/ - TorProject Archive
http://p3igkncehackjtib.onion/ - TorProject Media
http://kbhpodhnfxl3clb4.onion - Tor Search
http://cipollatnumrrahd.onion/ - Cipolla 2.0 (Italian)
http://dppmfxaacucguzpc.onion/ - TorDir - One of the oldest link lists on Tor

Marketplace Financial

http://torbrokerge7zxgq.onion/ - TorBroker - Trade securities anonymously with bitcoin, currently supports nearly 1000 stocks and ETFs
http://fogcore5n3ov3tui.onion/ - Bitcoin Fog - Bitcoin Laundry

http://2vx63nyktk4kxbxb.onion/ - AUTOMATED PAYPAL AND CREDIT CARD STORE
http://samsgdtwz6hvjyu4.onion - Safe, Anonymous, Fast, Easy escrow service.
http://easycoinsayj7p5l.onion/ - EasyCoin - Bitcoin Wallet with free Bitcoin Mixer
http://jzn5w5pac26sqef4.onion/ - WeBuyBitcoins - Sell your Bitcoins for Cash (USD), ACH, WU/MG, LR, PayPal and more
http://ow24et3tetp6tvmk.onion/ - OnionWallet - Anonymous Bitcoin Wallet and Bitcoin Laundry
http://qc7ilonwpv77qibm.onion/ - Western Union Exploit
http://3dbr5t4pygahedms.onion/ - ccPal Store
http://y3fpieiezy2sin4a.onion/ - HQER - High Quality Euro Replicas
http://qkj4drtgvpm7eecl.onion/ - Counterfeit USD
http://nr6juudpp4as4gjg.onion/pptobtc.html - PayPal to BitCoins
http://nr6juudpp4as4gjg.onion/doublecoins.html - Double Your BitCoins

http://lw4ipk5choakk5ze.onion/raw/4588/ - High Quality Tutorials

Marketplace Commercial Services
http://6w6vcynl6dumn67c.onion/ - Tor Market Board - Anonymous Marketplace Forums
http://wvk32thojln4gpp4.onion/ - Project Evil
http://5mvm7cg6bgklfjtp.onion/ - Discounted electronics goods
http://lw4ipk5choakk5ze.onion/raw/evbLewgkDSVkifzv8zAo/ - Unfriendlysolution - Legit hitman service
http://nr6juudpp4as4gjg.onion/torgirls.html - Tor Girls
http://tuu66yxvrnn3of7l.onion/ - UK Guns and Ammo
http://nr6juudpp4as4gjg.onion/torguns.htm - Used Tor Guns
http://ucx7bkbi2dtia36r.onion/ - Amazon Business
http://nr6juudpp4as4gjg.onion/tor.html - Tor Technology
http://hbetshipq5yhhrsd.onion/ - Hidden BetCoin

http://cstoreav7i44h2lr.onion/ - CStore Carded Store
http://tfwdi3izigxllure.onion/ - Apples 4 Bitcoin
http://e2qizoerj4d6ldif.onion/ - Carded Store
http://jvrnuue4bvbftiby.onion/ - DataBay
http://bgkitnugq5ef2cpi.onion/ - Hackintosh
http://vlp4uw5ui22ljlg7.onion/ - EuroArms
http://b4vqxw2j36wf2bqa.onion/ - Advantage Products
http://ybp4oezfhk24hxmb.onion/ - Hitman Network
http://mts7hqqqeogujc5e.onion/ - Marianic Technology Services
http://mobil7rab6nuf7vx.onion/ - Mobile Store
http://54flq67kqr5wvjqf.onion/ - MSR Shop
http://yth5q7zdmqlycbcz.onion/ - Old Man Fixer's Fixing Services
http://matrixtxri745dfw.onion/neo/uploads/MATRIXtxri745dfwONION_130827231336IPA_pc.png - PC Shop

http://storegsq3o5mfxiz.onion/ - Samsung StorE
http://sheep5u64fi457aw.onion/ - Sheep Marketplace
http://nr6juudpp4as4gjg.onion/betcoin.htm - Tor BetCoin
http://qizriixqwmeq4p5b.onion/ - Tor Web Developer
http://vfqnd6mieccqyiit.onion/ - UK Passports
http://en35tuzqmn4lofbk.onion/ - US Fake ID Store
http://xfnwyig7olypdq5r.onion/ - USA Citizenship
http://uybu3melulmoljnd.onion/ - iLike Help Guy
http://dbmv53j45pcv534x.onion/ - Network Consulting and Software Development
http://lw4ipk5choakk5ze.onion/raw/4585/ - Quick Solution (Hitman)
http://nr6juudpp4as4gjg.onion/tynermsr.htm - Tyner MSR Store

Hosting

http://matrixtxri745dfw.onion/ - Image Uploader

http://lw4ipk5choakk5ze.onion/ - PasteThis - Tor based Pastebin
http://wzrtr6gpencksu3d.onion:8080/ - Gittor
http://nr6juudpp4as4gjg.onion/ - Free hosting
http://tklxxs3rdzdjppnl.onion/ - Liberty's Hackers Hosting Service
http://matrixtxri745dfw.onion/ - Matrix Trilogy

Blogs

http://74ypjqjwf6oejmax.onion/ - Beneath VT - Exploring Virginia Tech's Steam Tunnels and Beyond
http://76qugh5bey5gum7l.onion/ - Deep Web Radio
http://edramalpl7oq5npk.onion/Main_Page - Encyclopedia Dramatica
http://ih4pgsz3aepacbwl.onion/ - Hushbox
http://ad52wtwp2goynr3a.onion/# - Dark Like My Soul
http://tns7i5gucaaussz4.onion/ - FreeFor
http://gdkez5whqhpthb4d.onion/ - Scientology Archive

http://newsiiwanaduqpre.onion/ - All the latest news for tor
http://5vppavyzjkfs45r4.onion/ - Michael Blizek
http://7ueo7ahq2xlpwx7q.onion/ - AYPSELA News
http://7hk64iz2vn2ewi7h.onion/ - Blog about Stories
http://tigas3l7uusztiqu.onion/ - Mike Tigas
http://mpf3i4k43xc2usxj.onion/ - Sam Whited
http://7w2rtz7rgfwj5zuv.onion/ - An Open Letter to Revolutionaries
http://3c3bdbvhb7j6yab2.onion/ - Totse 2
http://4fvfamdpoulu2nms.onion/ - Lucky Eddie's Home
http://nwycvryrozllb42g.onion/searchlores/index.htm - Fravia's Web Searching Lore
http://newsiiwanaduqpre.onion/ - OnionNews - Blog about the onionland

Forums and Chans
http://2gxxzwnj52jutais.onion/phpbb/index.php - Onion Forum 2.0 renewed

http://3fyb44wdhnd2ghhl.onion/ib/ - Onii-Chan
http://bx7zrcsebkma7ids.onion - Jisko
http://npdaaf3s3f2xrmlo.onion/ - Twitter clone
http://jv7aqstbyhd5hqki.onion - HackBB - Hacking & cracking forum
http://xdagknwjc7aaytzh.onion/20/http/1.4.7.9/forummain.htm - Read only access to the Freenet FMS forums via the Anonet Webproxy
http://sbforumaz7v3v6my.onion/ - SciBay Forums
http://kpmp444tubeirwan.onion/ - DeepWeb
http://r5c2ch4h5rogigqi.onion/ - StaTorsNet
http://hbjw7wjeoltskhol.onion - The BEST tor social network! File sharing, messaging and much more. Use a fake email to register.
http://t4is3dhdc2jd4yhw.onion/ - OnionForum 3.0 - New Onionforum for general talk, now with marketplace
http://zw3crggtadila2sg.onion/imageboard/ - TorChan - One of the oldest chans on Tor

Email and Messaging
http://bitmailendavkbec.onion - Swiss email
http://365u4txyqfy72nul.onion/ - Anonymous E-mail service. You can only communicate with other users currently using this service. So tell all your friends about it!
http://sms4tor3vcr2geip.onion/ - SMS4TOR - Self destructing messages
http://notestjxctkwbk6z.onion/ - NoteBin - Create encrypted self-destructing notes
http://torbox3uiot6wchz.onion/ - [TorBox] The Tor Mail Box
http://u6lyst27lmelm6oy.onion/index.php - Blue matrix chat NOT UP ALL THE TIME so chek often to see when it is
http://wi7qkxyrdpu5cmvr.onion/ - Autistici/Inventati
http://u4uoz3aphqbdc754.onion/ - Hell Online

Political
http://6sgjmi53igmg7fm7.onion/index.php?title=Main_Page - Bugged Planet
http://faerieuaahqvzgby.onion/ - Fairie Underground

http://2r2tz6wzqh7gaji7.onion/ - Kavkaz Center
http://tnysbtbxsf356hiy.onion/ - The New Yorker Strongbox
http://duskgytldkxiuqc6.onion/ - Example rendezvous points page
http://rrcc5uuudhh4oz3c.onion/ - The Intel Exchange Forum. Information and discussion on various topics, ranging from Illegal Activities and Alternative Energy, to Conspiracy Theories and Hacking. Same people from SnapBBS on a fully secure, moderated and categorized forum.
http://opnju4nyz7wbypme.onion/weblog/index.html - A7B blog :: a blog dedicated to the restoration of a limited constitutional republic in the USA
http://assmkedzgorodn7o.onion/ - Anonymous, safe, secure, crowdfunded assassinations.
http://duskgytldkxiuqc6.onion/comsense.html - Commo Sense by Thomas Paine
http://nwycvryrozllb42g.onion/ - Destination Unknown
http://zbnnr7qzaxlk5tms.onion/ - Wiki Leaks

Hacking

http://salted7fpnlaguiq.onion/ - SALT
http://yj5rbziqttulgidy.onion/ - Itanimulli
http://bbxdfsru7lmmbj32.onion/marketplace/ - Delta Initiative
Warez
http://2gxxzwnj52jutais.onion/ - The Nowhere Server (restored from backup after FH)
http://jntlesnev5o7zysa.onion/ - The Pirate Bay - Torrents
http://am4wuhz3zifexz5u.onion/ - Tor Library - library of books and other media files
http://uj3wazyk5u4hnvtk.onion/ - The Pirate Bay - Torrents (official .onion)
http://doxbindtelxceher.onion/ - DOXBIN
http://wuvdsbmbwyjzsgei.onion/ - Music Downloads
http://lolicore75rq3tm5.onion/ - Lolicore and Speedcore Music
http://xfmro77i3lixucja.onion/ - ebooks
http://vt27twhtksyvjrky.onion/ - lol 20th Century Western Music Recordings and Scores

http://2ygbaoezjdmacnro.onion/ - Pony at Noisebridge
http://xfmro77i3lixucja.onion/ - Imperial Library of Trantor
http://c3jemx2ube5v5zpg.onion/ - Jotunbane's Reading Club

Non-English

http://germanyhusicaysx.onion - Deutschland im Deep Web - German forum
http://ffi5v46ttwgx3fby.onion/ - Das ist Deutschland hier 2.0 - German Board
http://paisleli66axejos.onion/ - PAIS
http://runionv62ul3roit.onion/ - Russian Onion Union
http://s6cco2jylmxqcdeh.onion/ - ?ltimos bumps
http://5xki35vc4g5ts6gc.onion - GTF Greek Tor Forum . For greek speaking users
http://cipollatnumrrahd.onion/index.php - Cipolla 2.0 - Italian Community
http://runionv62ul3roit.onion - Russian community: market and anonymous talks about security, guns etc.
http://ptrackcp2noqu5fh.onion/ - PoliceTrack - Ne vous faites plus suivre par la police.

http://amberoadychffmyw.onion - Amberoad - russian anonymous market
http://r2d2akbw3jpt4zbf.onion - R2D2 - russian anonymous market
http://ramp2bombkadwvgz.onion - RAMP - biggest russian market (drugs only)
http://szmyt4v4vjbnxpg3.onion/ - Славянский
http://o2tu5zjxjlibrary.onion/ - Bibliotheca Alexandrina
http://xzzpowtjlobho6kd.onion/wordpress/ - DeepBlog
http://zqiirytam276uogb.onion/ - Thorlauta
http://ocbh4hoqs37unvv6.onion - French Deep Web

6. Secure Communications

Thanks to the recent revelations of Edward Snowden, people are becoming increasingly concerned about eavesdropping, official and otherwise. There are now many excellent apps and programs for all devices that enable secure communication. Recommend programs are listed below.

However, if your device is ever stolen or compromised by malware, the perpetrator will have access to all your encrypted communication tools. Therefore, it is often preferable to access ones' email, for example, via a Web portable rather than a dedicated email reader installed on the device. The same applies to texts and other forms of messaging.

People communicate on the hidden networks in much the same way as they do on the regular Internet. Personal messaging and texting are likely to overtake email as the preferred form of communication and this is reflected on Tor.

For secure email, use Tor or a Virtual Private Network (VPN) and sign up anonymously with a web-based free email service. The compendium of *clearnet* email providers on the Hidden Wiki has a detailed and current list recommended by Tor users <!> http://zqktlwi4fecvo6ri.onion/wiki/index.php/Main_Page#Email_.2F_Messaging.

If you need to send an email that positively cannot be traced back to you, there are numerous email re-mailing services on the Surface Web such as AnonyMouse. Re-mailers strip off any codes that identify you and add new ones along a multiple journey. When the email arrives at its destination, it cannot be traced back to you. This, of course, means they cannot reply. However, you can then give them an alternative means of contact.

A very simple option is to open a free email account with a company employing good encryption and privacy such as unseen.is and then give the address and log-in details to the other party. Messages are then written but saved as *Drafts* and never sent. The draft messages are then accessed by those with the password. This way the emails are never actually transmitted so are not easily intercepted. Be sure to change addresses regularly as over-active *Draft* boxes can arouse suspicion.

7. Secret Messaging

BitMessage Mail Gateway, is a Swiss-based Tor email service <!> http://bitmailendavkbec.onion/. A Surface Web option is unseen.is, an Icelandic-based free and subscription service offering 4096-bit encrypted email, chat, VoIP and file sharing. Another secure Swiss-based option is ProtonMail created in collaboration with scientists at Harvard, the Massachusetts Institute of Technology and the European research lab CERN. Cryptocat offers relatively simple encrypted chat for most Surface Web browsers. The latest version also works on Facebook.

Sigatnt <!>
http://sigaintevyh2rzvw.onion/ — Dark Net email system that masks identity and location of sender.

TorBox <!>
http://torbox3uiot6wchz.onion/ — Hidden email service only accessible via Tor.

PrivNote — free Surface Web-based service that allows you to send top secret notes over the Internet. Requires no password or registration. Write a note and it will generate a link. Copy and paste the link into an email or PM and send. The recipient then clicks the link to see the note in their browser. The note then automatically self-destructs which means no one can read the note again, and the link dies. You can choose to be notified when your note is read.

SMS4Tor <!>
https://www.reddit.com/domain/sms4tor3vcr2geip.onion/ - just like PrivNote but on Tor.

SpamMimic — Free online tool that converts simple messages into *spamtext*, the kind of weirdly-written junk that arrives in everybody's email box and therefore looks totally innocuous. Simply compose a short message, hit the *Encode* button and out comes a load of nonsense which you cut and paste into an email. The recipient then pastes the *spamtext* into the *Decode* box and out comes the original message.

8. Usenet Newsgroups

Newsgroups are rich source for all manner of media files that other people have posted that can be downloaded without drawing attention. They are also ideal for surreptitious communications.

There are Usenet apps for Android, iOS and Blackberry.
Newsgroups are rather like a vast bulletin board where anybody can post on any subject and anybody else can read those messages and download attachments. You need special Newsreader software and a low-cost subscription to the network. Usenet – which remarkably has been around since 1980 – has been largely ignored by Internet users probably because it does not have the same glitzy appeal of the World Wide Web but rather resembles an endless list of discussion topics, which is precisely what you do see.

During the 1991 coup attempt in Russia to oust President Gorbachev, activists used Newsgroups to get news in and out of the country and to communicate secretly among themselves.
Usenet is Deep Web and it is secure if you take the right precautions. It can defeat Deep Packet Inspection because it prevents the ISP from seeing inside the data by using secure 256-bit SSL encryption. Although your ISP can tell if you are accessing Usenet, once you pass beyond the curtain, everything you do there is hidden from inspection.

There are Newsgroups devoted to every conceivable subject from *alt.fan.jackie-chan* and *alt.aviation.jobs* to *alt.binaries.sounds.mp3.world-music*.

A network subscription costs US$4.99 per month upwards and gives access to an enormous store of digital material going back years, offering a better option than torrents for downloading without drawing attention. To see what is available, visit the search engine at binsearch.info.

A popular provider is Giganews http://www.giganews.com/ with bundled Mimo newsreader and add-ons.

It is always a good idea to use a VPN for all your online activities as it masks you from your local ISP allowing you to access Tor or the Newsgroups without anyone knowing.

Downloading from Usenet is secure, in that nobody can see what you are doing. Uploading sensitive material is slightly more risky and requires extra layers of security. For this, you will need to implement the following steps:

Do not use credit cards or PayPal when signing up with a Usenet provider. Many will accept the BitCoin or pre-paid credit cards, leaving you free to write what you like in the contact details.
Add a free VPN or one that accepts BitCoins to mask your activities from your ISP.

Sign up using Tor or the VPN so they cannot see where you are coming from (but do not combine Tor and Usenet access as this places strain on the Tor network).

Avoid signing up with any companies based in the United States.

Rather like placing a cryptic notice in *The Times*, messages can be sent and received by placing them inside any group you like, preferably the dullest possible. By placing your message in the group *alt.emircpih.pets.porcupines* and giving it a header that no one will want to open such as *Spam-Buster Pro*, you will have placed a needle inside the vastest of all possible haystacks that nobody without prior knowledge will ever be able to find.

9. Portable Apps

To keep sensitive data off your portable devices – documents, books, films, programs, etc – one option is to combine a secure Cloud service with a portable Operating System. There are an increasing number of Cloud stores now promising security and anonymity, options include Tresorit and Seafile.

Using the Tor browser on your device, open a Cloud account. Do not tie it with your real name or any banking details. Install on the Cloud the Platform portable operating system. Then install everything you need to access while on the go and the tools with which to access the data. You can also access this stored data from any device.

By only keeping a VPN or Tor on your device, there is nothing incriminating on your person and you can hand over encryption keys without fear of giving anything away. You just need to memorize the Cloud store location and login – accessing via the Tor browser.

Great tools freely available at PortableApps.com include:
Notepad Portable Text Editor, with support for multiple languages.

- VLC Media Player Portable.
- IrfanView Portable, graphic viewer for Windows. View pictures, vector graphics, animated images, movies, icon files, etc.
- GIMP Portable, Windows image editor.
- Sumatra PDF Portable, lightweight PDF viewer.
- Eraser Portable, securely delete files and data.
- 7-Zip Portable, portable version of 7-Zip. Works with compressed 7z, ZIP, GZIP, BZIP2, TAR, and RAR files.
- AVG Anti-Virus Free.
- McAfee Stinger Portable, common virus and 'fake alert' remover.
- Spybot Search & Destroy Portable, Spyware detection and removal.
- CamStudio Portable screen recorder.
- Command Prompt Portable.

- Download with DownThemAll.

10. 007 Apps

Scramble Calls — Silent Phone (https://www.silentcircle.com) for Android and iOS provides HD quality securely-encrypted phone/video communication over any network – 2G, 3G, 4G, WiFi. RedPhone (http://www.whispersystems.org) offers end-to-end encryption for Android. Signal from Open Whisper Systems is a free version of Redphone providing end-to-end encrypted text and VoIP calls for iOS and Android. Highly rated but needs tweaking to make it as safe as possible. See the configuration guide at DeepDotWeb. Unseen has also introduced a secure audio and video conferencing facility that promises high end security.
Jitsi is a free, open-source VoIP service for audio/video and chat that supports protocols such as SIP, XMPP/Jabber, AIM/ICQ, Windows Live, Yahoo!

Secret Messenger — there are secret messaging systems for all devices. Secret SMS for iOS will encrypt messages between users and hide them. Perzo is a new encrypted messaging system for all devices. There is also Signal Private Messenger for Android. SureSpot is an encrypted messaging system for Android and iOS that also allows you to send photos and audio clips. Delete a message and it is also deleted on the recipient's phone. Telegram is a free, open-source messaging app for Android and iOS with end-to-end encryption and a self-destruct feature.

Secret Image — Top Secret Video Recorder for Android and iOS allows you to seemingly switch off the smartphone while continuing to film. A quick examination of the phone will not show any activity. You can also make and receive calls while the camera is secretly running. ReconBot for Android is a stealth video, photo and audio recorder that displays a black screen while it records. Includes remote view so you can watch the recording live via a web link. Also includes location data.

Remove Image Data — if you want to upload images that cannot be traced back, you need to remove or alter the EXIF data which most modern cameras implant in the image to give GPS location and other details. Options for Android include the ExifEraser and ViewExif for iOS. 'Geotagging' can be turned off in most Android and Apple mobile devices by going into the *Settings*.

Secret Audio — there is Secret Voice Recorder for Android and Spy Recorder for iOS which can also automatically record when you enter certain locations that you set with Google Maps. The Top Secret Audio Recorder for iOS is a covert recorder that looks like a regular picture-viewing app. You can swipe through the photos but as soon as you tap on an image the recording begins. The recordings can also be password protected.

Record Calls — Top Secret Call Recorder for Android and various versions for iOS.

Ear Spy — convert your smartphone into a covert listening device by amplifying the sound around you. With Bluetooth headphones you can also leave your device in one room and listen in while in another. Free and paid-for versions for Android and iOS.

Confirm Contacts — if you receive a call and want to know who actually called, add them to a *Contacts* file and check them out with Contact Spy for Android and iOS which lets you quickly search people or companies by running them through this search engine app for web entries, images, news, blogs and US-only physical addresses.

Secret Compartment — secret folders for Android and iOS. Protect sensitive data by storing it in a hidden and encrypted file.

Location Trackers — helpful for dangerous assignments, GPS tracking allows for real-time monitoring of a phone's location via Google Maps. Some, like GPS Tracking Pro for Android and iOS, have a check-in feature so you can let the office know you are okay. Also highlights nearby safety points like hospitals.

Panic Button — Amnesty International has introduced an app disguised as a calculator that automatically issues a call for help when the user repeatedly presses the 'On' button, sending SMS distress messages to three previously-set destinations. Currently only available for Android.

See in the Dark — enhanced night vision photography and live feeds with the Night Vision Camera for Android and iOS. Works best on cameras with a good-quality lens.

Police Scanner — there are several police and emergency service scanner apps. Police Scanner for Android taps into scanners from around the world. For iOS, Radio Police Scanner does much the same.

Track Planes — Plane Finder – Live Flight Status Tracker for iOS and Android displays thousands of flights globally using real-time ADS-B signals used by aircraft to transmit their positional data. Enter flight number or tap on the map showing the planes above your head.

Chart Vessels — monitor the position of all manner of vessels from passenger and cargo ships to yachts and gin-palaces. Ship Finder – Live Vessel Tracking for iOS and Android picks up AIS position data from around the world and provides details and photographs of the vessels.

Mobile VPN — to cover your back, there is Hotspot Shield which encrypts all smartphone and tablet traffic through a Virtual Private Network (VPN) to mask your identity and prevent tracking (not recommended for use with Tor because it puts strain on the network). It also allows you to view banned content and access Twitter and Facebook mobile if their services are ever blocked locally.

Wipe Clean — Complete Wipe is an Android app that securely wipes a phone of sensitive data at the click of a button.

Remove Evidence — there are shredders for Android and iOS.

Self-Destruct — perhaps the ultimate weapon in Q's arsenal is the self-destruct feature. The free Wickr app allows you to encrypt any data – text, pictures or videos – and then have them self-destruct once unscrambled and viewed, leaving no trace for the forensic investigator. Available for Android and iOS.

Additionally, there is now a regular Firefox browser for both Android and iOS. Use this in preference to the browser that came bundled with your device. Also, install various security apps from within the Mozilla domain.

11. IP Cameras

Modern surveillance cameras use the same technology as any web-enabled device to stream video directly onto a network and, if you know the IP address, you can access the camera on a smartphone or any Internet computer.

Curiously, many cameras are not password-protected; this is especially true of those on private property which often provide street views. Some even have Pan Tilt Zoom functionality which allows anyone to zoom in and out and move the camera around. To access a specific camera you need to know its IP address. A quick Google search will provide live views of cities globally, or visit earthcam.com and control the cameras on Times Square and thousands of other locations.

Better yet, check out the Shodan search engine for the Internet of Things. Here are thousands of links to Internet-connected devices – many of them accessible without a password – including private and public IP cameras.

Tracking down cameras is not necessarily easy but can be done with time and patience. Google has a list of search strings to help you pinpoint cameras.

For newsgathering, IP camera smartphone apps offer the ability for live visual contact and coverage of events. A reporter armed with a smartphone and webcam app like SpyWebCam Pro for Android or Live Cams Pro for iOS can stream a live feed which can then be monitored back at base or by others in the field with mLiveCams for Android or IPCamSoft for iOS.

12. How to Search

To search the Internet effectively you need to know where to look, how to phrase your question and how to refine the search, so it helps to understand the main types of search service out there and how they work.

As obvious as it might seem, Web searching is a matter of selecting the right words and devising a strategy to find what you are looking for.

Unfortunately, not all search engines use the same rules but it helps to understand the basic way most engines work. Google, for example, uses Boolean logic, as do many of the popular engines. The examples below show how to refine any search and will work for most engines.

Getting the Most out of Search Engines

Phrase Search — by putting double quotes (" ") around a set of words, a Boolean engine knows to consider the exact words in that exact order. An example might be "fish and chips" which will show all documents containing that same phrase (12 million results), rather than all documents containing the word *fish* and all documents with the word *chips* (40 million results). Engines tend to ignore the word *and* when lower-case because it is too common to log.

You can also use double quotes to track down documents that you know contains a specific phrase, such as "Under the Federal Reserve Act panics are scientifically created".

By wrapping this sentence in quotes, Google and other Boolean engines will find around 20,000 documents containing a quote from 1929 by adventurer and Congressman Charles Lindbergh, whose baby son was famously kidnapped. This is effectively half the results if you had typed the sentence without the quotes.

This also works for names. The query "George Bush" will throw up over 70 million results, but take the quotes away and you have more than 225 million to choose from.

Do note that some search engines have a maximum limit of ten words so, if you are highlighting a particular quotation, select just ten of those words. Google recently increased its count to 32 words.

Excluding Words — a minus sign (-) immediately before a word tells the engine that you do not want pages containing this particular word. If you want to know more about Charles Lindbergh but want to remove all references to the kidnapping of his baby son in 1932, you would type "Charles Lindbergh" -kidnapping. This will reduce the results by about 200,000.

Some engines prefer the word NOT in place of the minus sign, such as "Airedale Terrier" NOT breeders (note Google prefers the – sign, while AltaVista is happy with either).

Wildcard — the asterisk symbol (*) tells the engine to treat the asterisk as a missing word and to come up with the best matches. Typing Google * will call up a list of all of Google's services from Google Translate through to Google Sky. The asterisk is also handy when looking for a word that has variants, like *smoking* but you would also like to see references to *smokers*, *smoke* and *smoked*. Try *smok**.

Using OR — by using the word OR in capital letters, engines can serve up a range of variables. To find a library or archive devoted to Lindbergh you would type "Charles Lindbergh" library OR archive and thereby widen your scope. Some engines prefer not to use OR but use the | symbol instead.

Using AND — another seemingly obvious one but something often neglected in web searches. By adding the uppercase word AND (or with some engines the + symbol) to a search phrase, specific elements are added to the search. Typing "Charles Lindbergh" AND economy will bring up results linking him with the economy. However, if we wanted to exclude results about fuel economy, we would add a minus sign: "Charles Lindbergh" AND economy -fuel.

Connections — use the underscore symbol (_) when looking for pairs of words that are directly connected, for example quick_start.

Search within a website — Boolean engines can be asked to search within a specific website for their results. Typing Afghanistan site:www.time.com will produce a breakdown of all references to Afghanistan in Time Magazine.

Domain Search — domains are broken down by country, such as *.af* for Afghanistan and *co.uk* for the United Kingdom, and by type of organization such as *.org* for non-profit making organization or *.edu* for education in the United States. Typing "hamid karzai" site:af will bring up everything listed on sites with an Afghan domain referencing the former President. Typing Afghanistan site:gov will return results only from a US *.gov* domain.

Search by Document Type — often, detailed information, especially studies and reports, can be found by seeking out particular document types. A request for Afghanistan filetype:PDF will offer only PDF files. Typing Afghanistan filetype:ppt will give results for PowerPoint Presentations, and *xls* for spread sheets. Be alert that certain files types – MS Word, Excel and PDF especially – may contain viruses and should be opened with caution. Where possible, use the *View as HTML* option within the search engine

Search Titles — many engines give you the option to search for keywords in the title of documents. intitle:Afghanistan AND landmines will take you to all documents with these two elements but these will also include news reports. Reduce this by typing intitle:afghanistan AND landmines filetype:ppt and you will be offered only PPP documents that contain these words in the title. Also be aware that different ways of spelling will influence the results, so you might want to type intitle:Afghanistan AND landmines OR "land mines". Using *allintitle* restricts results to documents containing all the keywords. For example allintitle:afghanistan drugs warlords.

Synonym Search — by inserting a tilde (~) in front of a word, most engines will search for the word and its synonyms. A search including the words *computer ~security* will also produce results covering encryption, malware, firewall, etc.

Search in URLs — website addresses (URLs) often contain clues to their subject matter, so you can seek out websites devoted to particular issues. For example, inurl:Airedale will offer websites purely devoted to the King of Terriers.

Related Site Search — using *related:* will bring up a short list of sites either similar to or in some way related or linked to a particular website, for example related:www.airedale.com.

Reverse Link Searching — websites and databases that you find particularly useful are often linked to by other equally interesting sites that you might also want to explore. To find out which sites link to the Internet Movie Database, for example, type link:www.imdb.com.

Cache Search — to search for sites and pages that no longer exist, typing cache:www.airedale.com will show the last stored version of that page. This is also particularly useful when researching sensitive subjects and not wanting to visit the actual website itself in case of malware implants known as "drive-by downloads" and the like.

Lucky Search — adding certain types of words to a search can produce interesting results, especially when you are looking for documents that may have been inadvertently posted online. These include "not for distribution", "company proprietary", "confidential", "secret", etc. Typing filetype:xls site:za confidential will produce several hundred pages of confidential business information from South Africa.

Number Search — to find numbers within a given range of things like prices, measurements and temperatures, separate numbers with two periods, like this shoes $30..$90.

Search by Date — not easy as most engines do not have a facility to date search, although Google does via the *Search Tools* tab. However, if dates do show up, they refer to the last time a particular page was indexed rather than created or modified. The ability to search by date is helpful as it allows you to weed out older documents and select the latest versions or search for news stories around a particular time.

You can type in *daterange:* and then the date but most engines operate on Julian Time, a scientific system of time measurement, so you will need a Julian Time converter. The date 7 July 2000, for example, appears as 2451733.06531.

To make matters worse, decimal points confuse most engines, so you have to drop the point and the last five digits. If we want to pin down the former Afghan president to a particular time-frame, say the first two days of April 2012, we would input daterange:2456019-2456020 Hamid Karzai (or Hamid Karzai daterange:2456019-2456020) and now we have just 13,000 results to choose from and a better chance of refining the search further. (Additionally, it may help on some engines to drop the quotes around phrases when using *daterange*.)

However, while this works for contemporary characters, it is less successful with historical ones. If we want to find out what Charles Lindbergh was up to between 20 May 1927 and 20 June that year, we would type "Charles Lindbergh" daterange:2425021-2425052. While this does narrow down the search, it is far from satisfactory as it includes many dates outside that range.

The Exalead search engine has a date search facility that allows you to search *before* and *after* dates, i.e. Mohammed Karzai before:2004/05/21 and Mohammed Karzai after:2004/05/21.

File Search

You can search specifically for PDF files via dedicated search engines:
- PDF Search Engine
- PDF Searcher
- Data Sheet
- PDF Geni
- PDF Database

PowerPoint presentations can be found via these engines:
- Slideworld
- SlideFinder
- JpowerPoint
- PPT Finder
- PPTSearch365

Where to Search

For the everyday things, Google and the conventional search engines do a good job. But detailed information is not always easy to find, especially when the engines throw up thousands of pages of results.

Most people rarely venture beyond the first page or two and after 14 minutes of fruitless looking even the most determined usually give up.

Understanding how to interrogate any search engine will certainly help. But knowing where to look is often more important.

The regular search engines only index a tiny fraction of the data stored on the Internet. They do this by extracting the 'visible' data on websites. This is then searchable with keywords.

But there is another world largely invisible to the conventional search engines. This is the Deep Web. This is not to be confused with the Dark Net – an area of the Deep Web largely concerned with illegal activities.

The information held on the Deep Web is generally contained inside databases and archives, and this content is not indexed by the conventional engines because they are rarely programmed to enter these data stores.

As such, this so-called Deep Web information can only be found by interrogating the database or archive directly through their own search facilities. The archives themselves can usually be found by asking a conventional Surface search engine to find them for you.

For example, suppose a Boeing 767 crashes and you want to look for similar incidents. You would begin your search in the conventional way with Google. But rather than asking Google to find the actual information itself, ask it to find a database dealing with air accidents, such as Plane Crash Info.

The data held within this site is, therefore, Deep Web because it will not have been indexed by the Surface search engines, so they won't know what is inside.

But, once at the database, you can directly enter the make and model of the aircraft, along with a daterange, and pull up every accident report for every incident globally, along with all the probable causes. Trying to do this by interrogating a Surface search engine alone would take more time than most people are ever likely to devote.

The same thing works for historical documents and quotations. For example, you may come across the line "I am the most unhappy man. I have unwittingly ruined my country" and want to pin it down. Google will certainly provide the apparent quote by Woodrow Wilson – *"I am the most unhappy man. I have unwittingly ruined my country. A great industrial nation is now controlled by its system of credit. We are no longer a government by free opinion, no longer a government by conviction and the vote of the majority, but a government by the opinion and duress of a small group of dominant men"*.

But what you see is not necessarily the actual quotation and you will also see endless examples of people regurgitating the line without pinning it down to a time and a place or to a specific document. You will also see a lot of debate as to its validity because most people do not know how to search effectively.

But, by knowing that Woodrow Wilson said this, Google can find the right archive, taking you to woodrowwilson.org where you can quickly track part of the line down to a 1912 campaign speech and find the remainder in the full-text version of Wilson's book *The New Freedom* published in 1913, the year he signed the Federal Reserve into existence.

You could spend all day on Google and achieve nothing, as opposed to 20 minutes reading in the right archive.

So it is not that difficult. You just need to know where to look and, of course, how to phrase the right question.

It would be difficult for this book to list every possible archive and database and all the other portals within the Deep Web, but below you will find some of the most useful. For the rest, ask a conventional search engine.

Search Engines – How they Work

Search engines work by storing key information from the webpages that they retrieve using an automated web browser known as a Crawler. This information is extracted from the site's title page, content, headings and meta tags. Results are generally presented in list form and can cover webpages, images and some file types. A few engines also mine data inside databases but coverage is a long way from comprehensive.

Some search engines like Google store all or part of the source page (known as a cache). Others, like AltaVista, store every word of every page they find. When a user enters a query into a search engine, the engine examines its index and provides a listing of best-matching webpages, usually with a short summary containing the document's title and sometimes some of the text. The engine looks for words or phrases exactly as entered.

Most search engines rank their results to provide the "best" results first. How a search engine decides which are the best pages tends to vary.

Most search engines are in it for the money and some charge advertisers to have their listings ranked higher. Those which don't charge make money by placing search-related ads alongside the regular search results and get paid whenever someone clicks on one.

Google Alternatives — Google, along with most search engines, stores detailed information about your interests. Each year, the FBI compels these companies to hand over the personal details of hundreds of users without presenting a court order. There are, however, alternative engines that do not store information on you in the first place:
IxQuick
Startpage
DuckDuckGo
Secret Search Labs

Deep Web Search — no single engine can search the entire Deep Web and no single directory can cover it all, but these go some way:

InfoMine — built by librarians at the University of California, California State University, the University of Detroit-Mercy, and Wake Forest University.

Librarians' Internet Index — search engine listing sites deemed trustworthy by librarians.

SurfWax — practical tools for dynamic search and navigation.

BUBL — catalogue of Internet resources.

Pinakes Subject Launch Pad — academic research portal.

Search.com — dozens of topic-based databases from CNet.

OAIster Database — millions of digital resources from thousands of contributors.

Metasearch Engines — a good way to perform a detailed search is to employ a metasearch engine to search multiple search engines simultaneously. These include:

DogPile

Mamma
Kartoo

Database Search — there are specialized search engines for finding databases. Arguably the best of the bunch is CompletePlanet which scours over 70,000 searchable databases and specialty search engines. Other notables include:
Search.com — seeks out databases and allows you to search multiple engines with a single query.
TheInfo.com — search specific engines and databases.
Beaucoup — one of the first specialized search engine guides, listing over 2,500 selected engines, directories and indices.
FinderSeeker — breaks searches down by country and even cities.
Fossick — covers over 3,000 specialized search engines and databases.

Repositories and Gateways
- Repositories of Primary Sources — direct links to over 5,000 archives, databases and websites globally.

- **WWW Virtual Library** — first catalogue of the web, started by Tim Berners-Lee in 1991. Run by a loose confederation of volunteers.
- **Librarians' Internet Index** — compiled by librarians offering a searchable, human-reviewed gateway to quality sites in the Surface and Deep Webs.
- **Digital Librarian** — a librarian's choice for the best of the web's databases and research resources.
- **GPO** — US Government Printing Office, access to multiple databases including records, hearings, reports, manuals, court opinions, etc.
- **Library of Congress Catalogs** — gateway to a vast collection of academic institutions, universities, libraries, and miscellaneous databases.

- CIA Electronic Reading Room — search for declassified CIA documents.
- Project Vote Smart — database of US government officials and candidates.
- USPTO — patient full-text and image database.
- US Census Bureau International Database — demographics, world population data, etc.
- WebLens — portal to academic and scholarly research papers and thousands of useful Internet research tools.
- DOAJ — Directory of Open Access Journals, free full-text scientific and scholarly journals, covering numerous subjects and languages.
- Geniusfind — directory of thousands of search engines, databases and archives organized into categories and subcategories.

- Ask Eric — education resources information center.

Open Directories — assembled by human beings who use editorial judgment to make their selections and not by Crawlers running algorithms. A web directory is not a search engine and does not display lists of webpages based on keywords but divides the web into categories.

The categorization is usually based on the whole website rather than one page or a set of keywords. Most directories are general in scope and list websites across a wide range of subjects, regions and languages. But some niche directories focus on countries, languages, industries, products, etc.

Popular directories include the Yahoo! Directory and the very comprehensive Open Directory Project.

User-Edited Directories — are compiled, as the name suggests, by users who are generally experts in their field and who wish to share favorite sites and improve search results. These include IllumiRate and JoeAnt.

Secret Searching

If you do not wish to leave any trace of your searches on your digital device there are various options.

Browsers — Arguably the most security-conscious browsers are Comodo's IceDragon for those who like Mozilla's Firefox and Comodo Dragon for those more familiar with the Google Chrome browser. Mac users should opt for Firefox.
You can switch between regular and private browsing by opening the settings. This will prevent your computer from logging your activities but it will not make you invisible. While Mozilla Firefox has a large number of free add-ons to help you beef up security, IceDragon has the edge.

Spend a few seconds tweaking with the *Settings*.
Select *Options/Privacy*. Tick the option *Do not tell sites anything about my tracking preferences*.
Under *Advanced/Network* tick *Tell me when a website asks to store data for offline use*.

Install the following free add-ons to improve security:

> **Force HTTPS** — Hypertext Transfer Protocol Secure (HTTPS) is used for secure end-to-end communication. HTTPS Finder for Firefox automatically detects and enforces HTTPS connections when available, providing a reasonable guarantee that you are communicating with the intended website and not an imposter, plus ensuring that communications between the user and site cannot be read or forged by a third party. The Electronic Frontier Foundation has its own free version HTTPS Everywhere for Firefox, IceDragon and Chrome browsers.

Kill Trackers — Blur (formerly Do Not Track Me) blocks web beacons and trackers that monitor browsing habits. Once installed, a tiny icon in the top right corner issues an alert whenever a site has a bead on you. Twitter and Facebook, for example, will try to insert trackers that follow you all over the Internet, allowing them to build a detail profile of your movements and interests. If people ever wonder how the social networks make money, this is how. There is also Disconnect Me which additionally offers a secure search facility.

Control Cookies — BetterPrivacy allows you to remove or manage cookies and gives various ways to handle Flash-cookies set by Google, YouTube, eBay and others. Privacy+ does much the same thing. Flash plugins run independently of your browser and bypass any proxy configurations. If you were trying to mask your identity, these will reveal your IP address which in turn will point to your physical address.

Java Switch — QuickJava allows you to quickly enable and disable Java, JavaScript and other intrusive plugins which track your location, travels and preferences. Other options include NoScript and Ghostery.

Cache Control — the Empty Cache Button adds a button to Firefox allowing you to quickly empty your browser cache should anyone start looking over your shoulder and optionally reload your page with just one click.

Avoid Detours — to stop websites opening other pages on your browser and taking you off to potentially harmful sites, try Redirect Remover which prevents redirects from links and images. Another good option is RequestPolicy.

Block Baddies — use either the free or paid-for versions of AVG or Avast which both warn of and block viruses and spyware entering your machine from malicious websites or the paid-for version of MalwareBytes (see Keeping out the Spies).

Secure Download — DownThemAll uses the browser's safety settings and so requires no configuration and features an advanced accelerator that speeds things up considerably. You can pause and resume downloads. It also allows you to download all the links or images on a webpage and customize the search criteria. It offers the ability to download a file from different servers at the same time for additional security. Privoxy is a web proxy service that fetches items (webpages, images, movies, etc) and passes them on to you when complete.

Safe Search Engines — obviously, Google keeps detailed records of your search queries so select an engine that won't store your records. Options include the Secret Search Labs engine, DuckDuckGo and iXQuick.

Cloaking — you can't beat cloaking your identity as one of the safest of all strategies. This way no one need know who or where you are. The simplest solution for quick, anonymous browsing is to use a facility such as AllNetTools, Guardster or Anonymouse. These free services allow you to type in any Web address and then travel around without leaving a trace of your activities or giving away your location. These are particularly useful for sensitive search engines queries and for visiting locally banned websites.

You can set up a proxy – which gives the impression that you are in another place – by fiddling with the *Settings* and changing the IP address to one provided by Proxy4Free or Rosinstruments but this can slow your machine down. A simpler solution is Stealthy, an add-on which seeks out the fastest proxies available and automatically routes you through them.

A more secure alternative is a Virtual Private Network (VPN), effectively a 'secret tunnel' where all your online activities are screened from the service provider and eavesdroppers. Free versions include FreeVPN and ProXPN. Mullvad offers a highly-regarded secure VPN service at comparatively low prices. They also accept payment in BitCoin for added anonymity.

It is always a good idea to cover the forward-facing camera on any device because you can never be certain if somebody is watching or not.

All this is good for general activity on the Surface Web but it is not 100% secure. It is safe to assume that if law enforcement or criminals want to monitor anybody's Internet access – read their emails and social media postings, harvest their contacts, find out what they are searching for and downloading, and listen in to their calls – then they can. This means that absolutely everything is open to inspection.

Search Sources

People Search — There are a range of specialty search tools for tracking down individuals. Most concentrate on the US but these will often pull up people from elsewhere on the planet, depending where they are listed.

Pipl — the best place to begin a search. Pipl casts a very wide net, searching within social networks, websites, blogs, magazines and newspapers, phone and public records, background checks, criminal records and even within classified advertisements. Works well internationally.

NameChk — once you have a person's social media username you can look for other instances of its use elsewhere on the Internet.

WebMii — find online public information. Good for finding physical and email address, plus phone numbers.

Yasni UK — free UK people search.

Yoname — good, across-the-board people search internationally.

LinkedIn — business-orientated social networking service, helpful for verifying individuals and for finding further leads.
Spokeo — primarily a US-based search facility with email and username search and reverse address and telephone look-up. Was once free, now charging for searches.
Abika — again, primarily US but very detailed search including criminal records by state, county and Federal, also global civil and criminal search, tax records, mortgages, evictions, background checks, personality profiles, traffic violations, vehicle history; plus image, audio and video search.
Zaba Search — also US but claims to offer three-times more residential listings than the White Pages. Also offers reverse phone lookup.
Public Records — a gateway to public records across the US.
Find County Records — directory of US county public records.
Jail Base — free and paid-for service offering jail inmate searches across the US.

123people.com — free international people search including social network usernames.

192.com — excellent paid-for people and business search in the United Kingdom.

Find My Past — search family records from Britain, Ireland, Australasia and the US. Subscription service.

UK National Archives — covers births, death and marriages, military records, employment, Census, etc.

Numberway — links to international White and Yellow page phone books.

FoneFinder — free, international reverse telephone number lookup.

CEO Email — find the personal email addresses of CEOs of UK companies.

Creepy — aptly-named free geolocation open-source intelligence (OSInt) tool that allows for target tracking using Twitter, Flickr and Instagram posts. Enter a Twitter user-name and see all the locations that the user has posted from, together with their Tweets and photo captions. Refine searches to location, time or date, and export to Google Maps for in-depth analysis.

GeoSocial Footprint — track peoples' haunts and locations using a combination of social media postings, GPS-enabled tweets, social check-ins, geocoding and profile harvesting.

Social Network Search

Topsy — excellent service which allows you to search for Twitter users across Twitter and other media, viewing their entire tweet timelines and references to them, etc. Also allows for date and language search.

Monitter — real-time Twitter search tool that allows you to monitor Twitter for mentions of any words or phrases, people, places or usernames, and from specific locations.

Facebook Directory — search people listed publicly on Facebook.

Social Mention — search trends across social networks and receive email alerts – covers people and celebrities, products, brands and companies, news events, etc.

Identify — Firefox plugin creates a profile of individuals' social media identities from any page.

Paid-for Search Services

Cision — comprehensive people watching service with real-time monitoring and analysis reports covering blogs, micro-blogs, social networks, forums, video and image-sharing sites, news sources, print and broadcast media. Track the impact of a story, identify key developments, trace individuals across the web.

Sysomos — business intelligence for social media, provides instant access to all social media conversations from blogs, social networks and micro-blogging services to forums, video sites and media sources.

Business Search

FT Search — search the Financial Times' archives, company profiles and business news with over 10 million full-text articles from 2,000 different European, Asian and American business sources. US$10 per month.

TechRepublic — the web's largest library of free technical IT white papers, webcasts and case studies. Covering data management, IT management, networking, communications, enterprise applications, storage, security, etc.
GuideStar — information on 640,000 non-profit organizations including recent tax returns.
Foundation Center — providing information on over 70,000 foundations, including grants. Look up organizations, identify funding sources, check statistics.
Kompass — search products, services and companies.

Economic Search
EconoMagic — links to over 400,000 data files with charts and excel files for each. Broad coverage including economic forecasts, indicators, reports, etc.
Free Lunch — free economic, demographic and financial data.
eFinancialBot — global search engine for financial resources.

Science and Engineering Search

Scirus — said to be the most comprehensive scientific research tool on the web. With over 545 million scientific items indexed, search for journal content and scientists' homepages, courseware, pre-print server material, patents and institutional repository and website information.

TechXtra — find articles, websites, books, industry news, job announcements, e-journals, e-prints, technical reports, research, thesis and dissertations.

E-Print Network — integrated network of electronic, scientific and technical information created by scientists and research engineers. All full-text searchable. Gateway to over 35,000 websites and databases worldwide, containing over 5.5 million e-prints in basic and applied sciences, primarily in physics but also chemistry, biology and life sciences, materials science, nuclear sciences and engineering, energy research, computer and information technologies.

Science Research — comprehensive public **SCIENCE** and technology research portal, searching over 300 collections globally.
Science.gov — search over 55 databases and over 2,100 selected websites from 13 Federal agencies, offering 200 million pages of US government science information including research and development results.
WorldWideScience — search portal to international science databases in multiple languages.
CiteSeer — database of technical and scientific literature sponsored by the School of Information Sciences and Technology at Penn State University.
NTIS — National Technical Information Service offers a keyword-searchable database of unclassified government-sponsored technical and scientific reports. Reports are downloadable and generally cost under $20.

Medical Search

MedBioWorld — resource portal for professional medical and biotechnology information.

UCLA Health — information resources for physicians and staff.

PubMed — comprises more than 22 million citations for biomedical literature from MedLine, life science journals and online books.

DrugBank — vast database of medicinal drugs.

Art Search

Musee du Louvre — find works at the Louvre, the Department of Prints and Drawings, and works in French museums.

Guggenheim — searchable database of selected artworks from the Guggenheim's permanent collection. The site contains more than 1,100 artworks by over 450 artists. Also includes works from the Peggy Guggenheim Collection Venice, and the Guggenheim Museum Bilbao.

National Portrait Gallery — more than 100,000 portrait records from the Catalog of American Portraits, a survey of American portraits in public and private collections across the US and abroad. National Portrait Gallery collections are included in this database.

Smithsonian National Portrait Gallery — find portraits for more than 80,000 people in this database.

Your Paintings — the entire UK national collection of oil paintings and the stories behind them. The digital archive is made up of paintings from thousands of museums and other public institutions around Britain.

Image and Media Search

Google Image Search — search over 880 million image files. Searches for keywords within the image filename, captions and accompanying text.

TinEye — reverse image search. Enter an image and see where it exists on the web.

Free-Ocr — extracts text from images which can then be run through Google Translate or other mapping resources.

Find Exif — reveal Exif data from images.
Foto Forensics — check to see if an image has been altered.
Internet Archive — superb digital library offering free access to books, movies, music and sound recordings, as well as 271 billion archived webpages. Includes the WayBack Machine for a snapshot of websites from different points in their past.
PicSearch — image search service with more than 3,000,000,000 pictures.
Yale University Library — access over 500,000 digital images.
Harvard University Library — vast historical image collection.
NYPL Digital Gallery — open access to over 800,000 images digitized from the New York Public Library's vast collections, including illuminated manuscripts, historical maps, vintage posters, rare prints and photographs.

Sonic — Library of Congress Recorded Sound Collection contains 2.5 million audio recordings on a variety of formats representing the history of sound recording from late 19th century cylinders and discs to digital files, include radio broadcasts and spoken word, as well as vocal and instrumental music.

BeeMP3 — search engine for locating mp3 audio files with over 800,000 in the database.

blinkx — vast video search engine.

MetaTube — browse 100 of the most popular video sharing sites simultaneously.

Miscellaneous Search

Public Library of US Diplomacy — searchable database of over 1.7 million US diplomatic files from 1973 to 1976, including diplomatic cables, intelligence reports and Congressional correspondence, courtesy of WikiLeaks.

The Spyfiles — WikiLeaks database of hundreds of documents from over 160 intelligence contractors in the mass surveillance industry.

Digital Public Library of America — over two million archived books, images, records, and sounds.
AgriSurf — agriculture and farming search site.
USDA — researchable database of all plant life in the USA.
FindLaw — search cases and legal news.
Galaxy of Knowledge — search the Smithsonian Libraries for digital content, books, images, etc.
EFF — the Electronic Frontier Foundation, protecting civil liberties in the networked world. On this site are white papers and a searchable archive.
CDT — The Center for Democracy and Technology is a non-profit public policy organization providing data on legislation affecting the Internet, works to promote democratic values and constitutional liberties in the digital age.
Project Gutenberg — searchable catalog of over 20,000 full-text books for free.
Internet Public Library — search resources by subject, newspapers and magazines, collections, etc.

US Census Bureau International Database — demographics, world population information, etc.

Genome — information on genomes including sequences, maps, chromosomes, assemblies, and annotations.

Europa Press Releases — find press releases from the European Union.

MagPortal — find individual articles from many freely accessible magazines, browse by categories or search facility.

Penn World Tables — international purchasing power parity and national income for 189 countries.

Aviation Accident Database — information from 1962 onwards for civil aviation accidents and incidents internationally. Generally, a preliminary report is available online within a few days of an accident.

US Zip Codes — online map of the US categorized by Zip codes.

Wolfram Alpha — computational answer engine providing direct factual answers and relevant visualizations. Discover weather details from a specific time and place, statistics and data analysis, people and history, socio-economic data, astronomy, and very much more. Well worth exploring.

Recommended Links

Avast - https://www.avast.com
Hotspot Shield - https://www.hotspotshield.com
Signal - https://whispersystems.org/
Smartphone Spy Apps - http://www.hongkiat.com/blog/iphone-spy-apps/
Ear Spy - http://www.overpass.co.uk/app/ear-spy/
Ship Finder - http://shipfinder.co/about/
Tresorit - https://tresorit.com/
Seafile Secure Cloud Storage - https://www.seafile.com/en/home/
FinSpy - https://wikileaks.org/spyfiles/files/0/289_GAMMA-201110-FinSpy.pdf
Fake Tweets - http://www.lemmetweetthatforyou.com/

Expand Short Links - http://checkshorturl.com/
No More Ransom - https://www.nomoreransom.org/
Angry IP Scanner - http://angryip.org/
Shodan - https://www.shodan.io/
Philips HUE lighting system - http://www2.meethue.com
Mozilla Firefox - https://www.mozilla.org/en-US/firefox/new/
Firefox Add-Ons - https://addons.mozilla.org/en-US/firefox/
Open Office Suite - https://www.openoffice.org/
VLC media player - http://www.videolan.org/vlc/index.html
Foxit PDF Reader - https://www.foxitsoftware.com/products/pdf-reader/
Recommended VPNs – https://www.deepdotweb.com/vpn-comparison-chart/
Tor Onion Browser - https://www.torproject.org/

Evidence Nuker - http://www.evidencenuker.com/
AnonyMouse Email Remailer - http://anonymouse.org/anonemail.html
Unseen Email - https://unseen.is/
PrivNote - https://privnote.com/#
PGP Pretty Good Privacy - http://www.pgpi.org/
Platform Operating System - http://portableapps.com/download
Recommended Search Engines - https://duckduckgo.com/ and see http://www.howtogeek.com/113513/5-alternative-search-engines-that-respect-your-privacy/
Newsbin - http://www.newsbin.com/
Usenet - http://www.usenet.com/
OpenStego - http://www.openstego.com/
Deepdotweb - https://www.deepdotweb.com/
Hidden Wiki - https://thehiddenwiki.org/

Also recommended:
http://www.wonderhowto.com/

Recommended Reading

**Deep Web Secrecy and Security
By Conrad Jaeger & Alan Pearce**

Deep Web Secrecy and Security is a MUST READ guide to protecting yourself against Big Brother for novice and expert alike, says the hacktivist group Anonymous.

The Internet was never conceived to be the preserve of commercial interests. It should not be a hunting ground for law enforcement. The time has come to take back control.

Everything you do on the Internet – every site you visit, every image or file you download, every email or message you send or receive – is logged on a computer somewhere. In a perfect world, we wouldn't need to worry. But this is not a perfect world.

Out there, someone or something is going through your personal data. From totalitarian regimes to outwardly democratic governments, there is a growing demand for access to people's personal data. They want to read your emails and they want to know who your friends are.

Personal information is a commodity today. It's bought and sold and analyzed, and then it's used to profile you for advertisers, campaign organizers, governments and criminals, stalkers and trolls. But none of this need happen.

You don't have to be up to no good to want to keep your on-line activities to yourself. Lots of people don't like having their mail read. Why can't ordinary people be anonymous, too?

'Deep Web Secrecy and Security' uses the secrets of the Deep Web to protect you and your family, your private and business interests, your views and your freedoms.

This book will show you in simple terms how to:
- Travel the Deep Web
- Protect Yourself On-line
- Set up Secure Communications
- Avoid Unwanted Attention
- Blog and Post Anonymously
- Access Banned Websites
- Erase & Protect your Activities

- Upload and Download Secretly
- Hide and Encrypt Anything
- Buy and Sell on the Parallel Internet

Deep Web for Journalists: Comms, Counter-Surveillance, Search
By Alan Pearce

Journalism has been transformed by the Internet and the Internet has opened journalists to levels of surveillance that would have horrified George Orwell. All journalists should be aware of the dangers they face in the digital world – the emerging battleground.

Being a journalist in 2017 is more dangerous than it ever was. In addition to the usual threats, beatings, murders and war casualties, we are now being actively targeted online by intelligence agencies, law enforcement and others.

These days it is not just journalists working in repressive regimes that need worry. We now know that the US and its cyber-allies – Britain, Canada, Australia and New Zealand – actively monitor domestic journalists in their mass surveillance of the Internet.

Edward Snowden has warned journalists that they are special targets and he has expressed surprise that news organizations rarely have any counter-measures in place.

They harvest our contacts and monitor our telephone logs. They read our emails and texts. They follow our every move online and they keep tabs on every line we write.

But it is not just intelligence agencies and law enforcement that we should worry about. All kinds of people have a vested interest in knowing about your next story – individual criminals and criminal organizations, political parties and extremist groups, law firms and the corporate giants.

Large business interests have their own intelligence units. They know what is being said about them and by whom. They keep track of their competitors and they know when somebody starts asking awkward questions about them.

If big business or anyone wanted to destroy a journalist's reputation this is simplicity itself.

The key is not to attract attention in the first place, and to learn to operate beneath the radar.

But how can journalists safeguard their sources and communicate without being overheard? How can they conduct sensitive research without having to watch their backs?

This book will show how to block intruders, set up secure communications, mask your identity online and browse and download anonymously, and store any amount of data without leaving a trace.

If that wasn't enough, the Deep Web is also a largely-unknown research and information resource. If you know the right entry points, you can mine a rich seam of multimedia files, images, software and documents that you cannot find on the Surface Web.

Deep Web for Journalists "offers an uncompromising diagnosis of the perils of online communications and should shatter the confidence many of us place in the unguarded ways of working online," says Jim Boumelha, President of International Federation of Journalists in his Foreword to the book.

Journalist, broadcaster and author Alan Pearce has covered conflicts from the Khmer Rouge to the Taliban for the BBC and Time Magazine, among others. He now teaches cyber-security skills and counter-surveillance to journalists.

"The work of journalism has become immeasurably harder than it ever has been in the past. Journalists have to be particularly conscious about any sort of network signalling, any sort of connection, any sort of licence plate reading device that they pass on their way to a meeting point, any place they use their credit card, any place they take their phone, any email contact they have with the source - because that very first contact, before encrypted communications are established, is enough to give it all away." – Edward Snowden 17 July 2014 in The Guardian.

Enter the Dark Net
By Conrad Jaeger & Alan Pearce

Do you want to visit the dark side of the Internet?

Out there – beyond the prying eyes of law enforcement – is a Secret Internet, a place where spies, master criminals, pornographers, journalists, terrorists and the super-rich can do what they like with total impunity.

This quick, inter-active e-book shows you how to dive straight into their world and explore the hidden depths.

Learn how to enter a gateway to the Dark Net using freely-downloadable programs and applications; how to mask your identity and travel the Surface Web with total anonymity, plus upload and download securely, send secret emails and messages, and leave no trace.

Explore the strangest websites, chat on the oddest bulletin boards and generally do what you like without having to look over your shoulder. With active table of contents and direct links to Hidden Networks.

Until now, finding your way in or navigating its depths has not been easy. In fact, it is positively dangerous unless you know how to proceed and it is all too easy to give yourself lasting nightmares. So be warned.

Direct links to the Hidden Wiki, Silk Road blackmarket, etc

Welcome to the Internet's greatest secret – The Dark Net.

Deep Search: How to Explore the Internet More Effectively
By Alan Pearce

Find what you're looking for in a fraction of the time. This enlightening and easy interactive ebook will improve your search skills; cutting the time you spend trawling the Web for whatever you want.

Learn how to get the best out of Google and the other search engines. Discover 'unknown' databases and archives.

Knowing Where to search if often more important than knowing How to search. This book shows both. With active links to the Internet's most useful search tools.

Discover how to search the Deep Web for documents, images, videos and forgotten gems of all kinds.

Learn how to mask your identity and research 'sensitive' subjects without giving away who you are or where you are.

The perfect tool for anyone who seriously needs to search the Internet – journalists, students, researchers, law enforcement and librarians.

Covers People Search, Social Media, Art, Science, Engineering and Country Searches, and much more.

The Sherlock Holmes Handbook for the Digital Age
By Dr John Watson & Alan Pearce

Sherlock Holmes is the greatest detective of all time. He is driven to right the wrongs of the world. It is only natural that he should turn his attention to the Internet.

"The Internet has become a sinister and dangerous place – a grotesque parody of all that it originally promised," explains Holmes. "Open your eyes, Watson. We are living in a postmodern surveillance dystopia from which escape for all but the most skilled individuals is impossible."

Luckily, Holmes has all the right answers. This is a cyber-security and digital counter-surveillance handbook like no other.

Our two heroes embark on a perilous journey to the Dark Side learning along the way to avoid the traps laid by their adversaries – the State, the Corporate Giants and the Criminals and Insane.

From self-destructing messages to anonymous browsing, we visit alternative Internets and discover how to employ the Dark Arts for the power of good.

This is a Call to Arms. The time has come to reclaim the Internet from the commercial interests, the scammers and the surveillance state. And – as Sherlock Holmes clearly demonstrates – it is really simplicity itself. This book may only take a few hours to read but it will change your life.

Books by Alan Pearce are available from all good online book stores including Amazon. Or visit www.alanpearce.com

Printed in Great Britain
by Amazon